Who's Watching You?

Who's Watching You?

DONALD JOHNSON

LitPrime
"Your story is our priority"

LitPrime Solutions
21250 Hawthorne Blvd
Suite 500, Torrance, CA 90503
www.litprime.com
Phone: 1-800-981-9893

Published by LitPrime Solutions   07/29/2022

ISBN: 979-8-88703-013-5(sc)
ISBN: 979-8-88703-014-2(e)

Library of Congress Control Number: 2022909492

Contents

Who's Watching You?

- A true story about the survival of a woman caught in the grips of a devil and surviving by jumping from a truck moving at over 55 mph.
- A resolution to help save others from such a tragedy by helping to introduce DNA testing into mainstream law enforcement. Soon after helping to catch the Baton Rouge serial killer.)
- A lawsuit to change the ways that pertain to security and personnel behind camera's.
- A trial that became a threat to the victim!!!
- Recovering by pure strength of character and love.
- A question to all who read this book!
- What would you have done?

As it is always hard to describe one's own life to others it is more so to write about another. Ellen Crawford as she was christened was born to parents who came to meet in a different county of which both parents were born. Their homes were in Jackson County, Tennessee, but moved from their because of harsh times. Moline (named for a tractor from Illinois) was tall & sturdy. She had one sister who was always jealous of her because as siblings are one more beautiful than the other. This showed its truth when Jr. Crawford saw Moline. Edna was always resentful of her because Jr. took favor of her sister.

Jr. courted Moline and in short time married. Nine months and one week later Ellen arrived. She was the first of eleven baby Crawfords to come to their marriage. (11/27/48).

Her first year was of love and care. Great pride from parents who wanted children but mom was already expecting child number #2. Birth control had not come to be a word of mainstream America yet. As the years went by the house soon filled with children. By age 7, Ellen had six siblings. By now, also since she was the oldest, she was given the responsibilities of a mother. She would diaper, feed, rock-buys all those that needed it from that early age to 18. She told me that each time her mother left for the hospital to deliver another child she dreaded and love it at the same time.

With each new occasion with a newborn in the house, there come unrest. Children who would have to double up to make room for another child to come in.

Ellen got more chores since she was the oldest. But she loved them all.

She told me of how they would all pile out of the car when they visited her grandparents. Her grandmother would cringe but grandpa loved it. He would show them his farm. The chickens and ducks and old Elder. Now Elder was her grandfather's pride and joy <u>white</u> <u>mule</u>.

Tenn sold a lot of males back in 40's & 50's. Lebanon TN (which is where she lived all her life) was well known for their auctions of high grade mules.

Elder was a top mules except staying out of the garden. Occasionally he would want a snack for all his labor.

Ellen always enjoyed the trip out to the country except one Sunday her father took ill and she was given the task of getting them all home safely as her mother couldn't drive and her father to sick to hold the wheel. So at 13 years old - 10 children and 2 adults got a chance to see Ellen drive down a bumpy grovel road 25 miles to home.

She said her mother kept screaming watch out for the mailbox - all the way home. All the kids were normally yelling and screaming but now quiet as lambs. Most of the girls were holding on to each other. She ran 3 stop signs that day. Scare half a dozen chickens and 2 dogs who thought they had the upper hand but turned tail when they saw what was coming. It had to be funny in the least.

Anyway she made it safely and never looked back till she thought about how it got her to mature so much earlier in life than she had to. She now was their strength to call on. She couldn't be a little girl <u>anymore</u>.

As the years went by the family grew up close. Often they would go to movies and watch as a group. One Saturday they went to see a movie that was so good everyone decided to watch twice. Well that didn't go well with Jr. He met them all in the theater and marched them home to their punishment for worrying him so much. That never happened again.

Meals were always a chore for her mother. She peeled 10 lbs of potatoes each and every day. This was a staple for the family. Her mother knew how to cook them to stretch it as far as it would go as there were rarely any leftovers. I had the fortunate opportunity of eating a Thanksgiving meal after Ellen and I met at her mothers home. "Don't be late" with over 40 people looking at a large turkey you need to get there early. But what a joy to see.

As Ellen grew older and more mature, her father guarded her well. Screened boys and made sure of who they were. She said he ran a few off over those days.

Now Jr. Crawford worked hard in the ornamental field. He built large gate entree's for several stars living over in Nashville especially???

He was also one of the best fiddle players in the region. Several people came to him for him to teach them. Also <u>Earl Scruggs</u> wanted him to go on tour back then with them but he declined because what mattered to him most was his family.

So life was pretty normal for Ellen as she adopted easily to lessing the chores to the children and looking out for herself. She loved music and books.

After graduation she worked for her father until age 23.* She then married Bill who was the son of wealthy parents but as some things go in marriage the other person soon forgets why they joined up with you and try to change you.

Bill had owned a spa and exercise center in Lebanon, TN. He was 10 years older. He had her instructing exercises at his spa now and expanded the business to 4 such spa centers. They traveled to promote the stores and she would do 6 or 7 sessions a day for each store.

She soon tired of the stress. The arguments. The brutal remarks. Time was getting short.

Her father suggested she try out for Miss Wilson. Take her mind off home life and her self esteem.

*She had never thought of a beauty contest for any reason. But as humble as she was she accepted the chance to be in one. Wilson County as all places have those who cherish such awards and it shook there foundation when she won over local rich family dollars and pull. She should have gone on to Hollywood. She had the look & figure to be in movies. Really.

She won hands down she thought because of her speech that all contestants had to give. She spoke of Viet Nam. It was always controversial but none more than at that moment. But she said that the most important part was that if we were in a war with people who wanted to "kill and conquer us" -

"Would we not want someone to come and help us." We must always stand up for those who can't."

She was given the prize of use of a limousine to Nashville for the day & there she was given the works at the best salon in Nashville. She loved it.

Fast forward in time: 5 yrs have past and a divorce did ensue. She couldn't continue as things were with no resolution. So for several years she worked and stayed to her family for support. God was always with her she said.

1990 - We met - That wasn't - We knew each others from the start. From that day on all our days were for each other. She soon moved in together and felt the world had finally changed toward a happy life. And it did.

But a year later, my company closed. No work no money. I sought work in my home state of La. and got a good offer. So we came South.

Life was good for us. Both working, making good money then.

3-11-2001 only 6 months before the attack on the World Trade Center and our great country. How awful for our fellow citizens and responders.

What happened to me was no less horrific. Every women's nightmare! But I survived to tell you my story; now through my husband.

I am gone now after all these years. I rarely spoke about it, though we lived it and its memories for years. Cancer took my body, kidney. Didn't know till the end. Blessed in a sense. Finally at peace now. No more bad dreams or nightmares to contend with.

It was a beautiful Spring Sunday morning. This week Don was offshore working on a drill ship in deep water. We always talked early in morning because communication was restricted for other company needs. I was told that my company supplies were low and I wanted to go that morning before crowds arrived after church. He had asked me to take his stepfather along with me who was next door but I assured him that having read literature that said statistically that Sunday morning at 9:00 was the safest time to shop because criminals slept in. He laughed. But I reassured him again. Statistics had reported such nonsense and it proved wrong.

So bravely or further concern & I drove the few blocks to the then largest retailers outlet. I knew they had camera's every where so I had no concern or even sense of danger to come.

The few supplies I had gotten rather quickly and now off to

the house I go. So I thought. I walked out knowing I should be on camera and someone surely was watching but don't believe it.

I saw another women ahead of me exit the store. Everything seems normal, I felt. As I walked out the automatic doors I watched the woman, who was then loading up her goods, casually close her trunk of her car.

I had but 20 feet more to go before I reached Don's truck. Opening the door I proceeded to load up the smaller bags and reached into the truck to do so.

Suddenly a sharp pain in my back then another and another. I was fainting. What was going on? Suddenly I was thrown into the passenger floor board and someone or something was forcing me down. I couldn't breathe. I couldn't move. All I could see was darkness. Then I felt someone grabbing my hands, ripping my diamond wedding band from my hand and tearing the keys from a wristband on the other wrist. Then finally I could catch a breathe. I saw the devil for the first time that day. He was dark as a moonless night and gold tooth. I reached for a can good and hit him directly on his head but it didn't faze him the least. He then hit me with force that knocked me down onto the floor again. He stabbed me in my arm as I tried to fight back but was hit again.

Moments passed. I was getting weak. Losing blood - the brute force upon me. I tried to get out but he stabbed me again in my back twice. I felt limp. He started the truck and pulled out to leave. I made another attempt, this time, to kick out the window of the door. As I did kick it twice he again stabbed me but this time in my thigh and deep. Blood flying everywhere. It took all I could do to stay conscious and try to stop the flow of blood leaving my body. It was all I could do now. Shock was taking over. As he drove thru the large parking lot he actually waved to the cameras. He knew they were there. Surely someone saw all this happening. Surely someone would come to my rescue. Surely, we found out later.

\- No one watches -

\- No one - No one -

All these camera's give you a false sense of security. A deterrent as such. A false belief that help would almost surely be there. Never believe that.

I could feel our movements through the city as he sped to get out of town. Finally I had stopped the bleeding in my arm but my leg still bleed heavily. Time seemed to stop and speed at the same time. I was so shocked that this could be happening to me. To me. We were now in an area I had never seen and asked it why. Why did you do this to me?

This was the first time I saw his face. I wanted to die. Here was a human with no soul. Badly dressed, gold tooth, smelling of alcohol, rough in nature as a wild man who had no care - then he told me. He had gotten out of the Louisiana State Penitentiary at Angola. This perpetrator had been released by the state under what was then called The Good Time Law - Yea. He had been sentenced to 7 years for aggravated robbery and attempted abduction. He worked as a cook - there-fore considered a model prisoner. He was eligible for reduction of term by half and set free. He was out two weeks. He never saw or contacted or called his parole officer. Always wondered why he had not been looked up by the officer himself. He said he had no money and saw the rings I had; and needed wheels. I felt faint again. It was then he pulled over and raped me. I fought but he hit me again. So I let my mind go somewhere else. I thought of my husband and I thought of the family.

I felt nothing. Somehow God let me not be aware of this attack. After his filthy deed he drove again. I wanted to die. How could I ever face my family, friends and husband. We drove for what seem like hours. Then he said - I've got to take you somewhere that will wash your body clean of my DNA. I know of the perfect spot near the Atchafalaya River Basin. No one would find you there and if they do they won't know who you are. How can someone speak of these things so openly as if he had done so before. Every minute that passed was one more that I lived but if I was going to die, it wasn't going to be by his hands.

I called upon my God. I had no more hope that I would survive this. I asked God to help me. To accept me as I was at this moment. Helpless, but still his servant. We now were getting into a more remote area. No longer seeing homes or vehicles. But as God always has a plan - I saw two men in a pasture up ahead next to a fence moving cattle.

It was then that I heard God's voice. He was clear and calming to me. It was a male voice who told me what to do. He assured me that I would be saved. I couldn't be sure of anything at this moment except I wasn't going to die. He told me to open the door with both hands at the same time. Not to worry about the fall. I trusted God all my life. No better time than now. I did as he said and pushed forward with what strength I had left.

The door opened and I dove for the opening. As I did I felt a grip on my bra and sweater pulling at me as firm a grip I ever felt. But the weight was too much for him to hold and drive. The last time I looked his way all I saw were gold teeth and evil. I knew we were traveling over 50+ mph. As I saw the road going by so fast, I knew this would hurt. I forced my way out.

-Darkness-

I was told I looked like a large doll tumbling down the highway. My angel cowboys saw what was happening at the last moment. They had come to my aide that morning unbeknowingly God knew this would happen. Three days before this chuck had gotten a flip phone. Never needed one he said and the reason they were there that morning was they had to move a herd of cattle to another pasture or they wouldn't have been at that spot.

As I tried to sit up now I saw the truck come to a screeching halt. Why no. He wants to run over me now. I had to move somehow. The pain was horrific. I couldn't move my arm. I couldn't move my leg. Blood in my eyes. Blood all over me. My long blonde hair now red and tangled. How can I run from this attack? I fell backward and rolled as fast as I could make my damaged body move. I heard the tires burning rubber as he was coming towards me. I wasn't sure I could do this but as I made the last roll I felt the truck's bumper just miss my head. Inches more or less could have changed this whole story. As it stopped again - I wondered if I could get out of the way of his next attack. But then he drove off.

And I then knew why. My angel cowboys had gotten there in time to scare him off. I supposed he thought he had hit me and left me for dead. I tried to stand up to scream to them but fell flat on my face.

As they got to me I could hear Rixby calling 911. Frantically he talked at first but soon calmed down. Both seemed so shaken by my sight. But I was alive. Thank God I was still alive.

The ambulance arrived first. Then half a dozen parish sheriff cars pulled up. As they put me on a stretcher I was asked to give all the information I could. I had memorized our truck's license and gave a description of him. But I wanted to call my husband more than anything at this time.

Rixby dialed the number and waited for someone to answer.

The phone rings. Little did I know how one call can change a lifetime of dreams into a nightmare. A stranger's voice asking me who I was and if I knew an Ellen Crawford Johnson. I said yes and he explained briefly who he was and the situation of the moment. Shock - What? - How? - Was she OK? He then handed her the phone. Though she was so badly injured and traumatized she could still speak calmly. She told me she was alright and in safe hands now and asked me to come home. We both cried. I told her I was coming if I had to swim. Treatment was on going as we talked. We had to shortened our conversation. Said our I love you's and hung up.

I had never know such fury to enter my heart. I raged about the control room and thru a door to the deck of huge drill ship. Tossing things and beating on metal railing in despair to get some relief from what I just heard. As this rage left me I knew I had to move to shore. But how. 100 miles of water between myself and shore. No boats except on standby. That would be a 12 hour trip back to land by seas. Fortunately that Sunday I had scheduled a helicopter for the field to run over to another platform for a well test but soon commandeered it for my use. It was due in 25 minutes. I was ready and headed in soon. The pilot and I flew in silence as I wanted to speed things up. I contacted shore and told them the situation and to check me off work list at shore. I soon hit the beach and started the next 90 miles to Ellen in my car. I drove frantically. Hoping to get stopped; to be given escort to her. But where was she now. I called sheriff's office and I was told she was still in route to the hospital. By the time I got there the parking lot was full of police cars. An ambulance was pulling in. I knew things were worse than what I was told.

As I entered emergency room area officers stopped me and questioned me. I explained who I was and escorted to her as quickly as we could go. Then I saw Ellen. Disbelief and reality both merged into one. Three nurses and a doctor were at her side. But like a real trooper she smile at me. Always she was concerned for others rather than herself. She wanted me to call the family. That was understood.

But how can I tell them. Which one should I call. She was the oldest of eleven children. Her mother was still with us then. Some one had to tell her. Deciding to call Harold, not the oldest but a minister gave me my best choice. He could gather them to go see her mother - together.

Ellen was the county queen of Wilson county Tennessee when she was 24 years old. She was admired by all her family and friends especially because of her heart. So kind to all. That's why I believe the devil couldn't stand to see her be happy. She had taught Sunday school as a young woman. She saved a family from a burning home in the middle of winter. She was always charitable. A soul so rarely seen anymore.

Four children arrived simultaneously at their mothers home. A mother knows when bad news comes. She just didn't know what.

As Harold tried to tell her - she knew it was Ellen who was hurt. She told them she was going to get there no matter what it took. They all came. Seventeen in the first wave. Then others came later.

I had to get back to Ellen then. She had seven stab wounds, a broken leg, a broken ankle in three places, a broken left wrist, upper left arm was broken and a hematoma the size of a grapefruit on that arm. Not to mention all the cuts and bruises from jumping. Looking at her made me realize how truly brave and strong she was. She never cried. She smiled at me. She said "God Saved Me Today."

We had to move Ellen to another hospital. She needed surgery. She also needed safe guarding. This animal was still loose. He might come back to finish the job he had started.

Under police escort she was transferred to a Lafayette hospital.

She was put in ICU for three days under guard. The swelling was so bad that surgery had to be postponed. Her room was full of flowers and balloons. Only those with clearance could see her.

By now the man hunt was on. I even joined in the hunt by driving around looking for my truck and whoever would be in it. A break came in a sighting by a female deputy. She saw him coming straight onward and as he passed her she knew it was him. (Ellen had picked him out of a nine person line-up of photographs) she turned as he sped off. Chasing the truck thru neighborhoods, she came upon it abandoned. But the net had already close in on him. Other sheriffs and city police locked down eight blocks on the hunt for him. A dog was sent to do the final hunt. He was found hiding in his mothers attic. She said he wasn't home but she knew the truth.

Angola - the most secure prison in Louisiana. Surrounded by swamp with snakes and alligators. The other barrier is the Mississippi River. No one escapes alive from here. But the Louisiana Legislature set a large population free because of a financial crises the state was facing at that time. How convenient for them. This was soon to change.

Ellen's recovery was slow. Seventy-seven days I slept on the cot next to her medical bed to give her comfort I was there. I wasn't going to abandon her. I knew what this would do. Most men would have turned their backs on this situation. Not being able to cope with the rape. But it wasn't her fault. I had to overlook that and see Ellen. Ellen who I loved and would stand by till the end of my days with.

Through those months we were visited by friends and law enforcements. One female officer was kind to Ellen. She too had been attacked and raped when she was young. This was her reason for being on the police force now.

We traveled with them trying to trace the route he took her on but to no avail. The trial was soon to come.

Now a year has gone by and court was set. We would have to endure a month of jury selection and testimony. It was DNA that had been taken from the vehicle that convicted him.

Along with other facts that she identified him and semen sample was found, the trial seemed to move smoothly.

Ellen was called to the stand to testify. I had dreaded hearing this in open court but I had to hear it again one more time.

Halfway during her personal accounting, I heard chuckling and laughter. Talking openly like it was a joking matter to someone. I looked over to see two women both cutting up as if at a comedy club. The judge stopped the Trial-Cold.

He ordered the bailiff to take the two women into his chambers. The trial stopped for 15 minutes. The judge came back and ordered a recess.

*Note must be made here because of the new to science - discovery and possible usage of DNA sampling at them that time in history. If not for the complete and logical testimony of the the then most fore-front scientist of DNA testing most people would not have believe its credibility. He got the job done!!

It was soon we found out what happened. The prosecuting attorney told us that the two were his relatives. One was his aunt and the other was a cousin who was a sheriff deputy in that parish. He fined the aunt $500 for contempt and told the deputy he would not accept any reports from her in the future, thus ending her career in law enforcement. As we resumed the trial 4 of the largest deputies stood besideEllen and I. We also found out his father was there but never returned. This had gotten everyone concerned. No more than myself for Ellen.

The DNA plus his weak alibi convicted him. It was stated that it had a 1 in 12 million chance of being someone else. Not likely. 2 female jurors cried during Ellen's open court testimony. He was also placed driving the truck by two others.

The jury was quite serious in their exiting of the court room. At this point it was all up to them. All the traveling for two weeks. All the hot days of concentrating on the court proceedings and testimony. It was all up to them.

Ellen and I waited with the prosecutor and the assistants to the DA's office next door to the courtroom and waited mostly in silence. It seem like hours. Never sure when one is in court.

The call was made. (Jury coming in) We all looked each

others way and nodded. We had already said our prayers in silence.

After we all got settled, the judge came in. The judge was openly concerned. He was meticulous about everything. He did not want a mistrial. After the jury returned with a conviction he wanted to sentence him soon. He gave him life + 40 years at Hard Labor with no possibility of parole - ever.

At the sentencing he was allowed to pass by unguarded near me. I wanted his neck in my hands but knew that it would do no good. Only harm to Ellen and I. I couldn't go to jail - who would watch over her? I was always concerned about depression taken over her life. She didn't want to drive every again or go any where alone. Never went outside alone ever again.

Soon after the trial we moved to the country. I had land there and bought a house - moved it and remodeled and settled in licking our wounds. Thanks to our good friends Mike and Toni who drove over 200 miles that day to help us get settled.

But we weren't done yet.

Soon we were asked because of this case to have Ellen make a statement to a gathering of state police and legislators. She was their poster child. By now the case had been all over TV and papers. Everyone now was aware of DNA test. But what hadn't happen was swabbing. The testing of DNA by swabbing of a person with a cotton swab after a crime or traffic violation was not law yet.

Ellen's concern was to help make sure that this would not happen again. It would be a deterrent to others to not commit a crime knowing this might catch them. We agreed. She stood before a very large crowd in Baton Rouge and told her story and how it confirmed her statements made in identifying her assailant. They applauded her. I saw tears. They know the tragedies oh so well but still feel pain also.

So it became law in Louisiana. The first to make it official at catching the bad guys.

*Just knowing that entering a place; a person leaves his or her DNA, should be enough for criminals to not do the crime.

Nov 22, 2002

We were contacted by state officials and the meeting was set. Little did she know it was the largest gathering of state officers and state troopers and high officials of the state.

Swabbing of all detainees for sexual assault or violent crime was conducted. This was new ground in testing of DNA. Previous usage was only on convicted individuals. So now anyone could be swabbed if suspected.

Soon afterwards at 1:30 AM a diligent employee at the DNA lab in New Iberia got a match on someone Baton Rouge was staring. The serial killer of Baton Rouge: Derrick Todd Lee.

* A swab was given to Lee at his home on May 5, 2003. His DNA matched those crime scenes

May 5 2003 at Lee's Home

His crime spree span from 1992-2003. He killed 7 women. He was only caught because he had been given a swab test. If not for the swabbing he could still be pouring cement in neighborhoods near you.

After the DNA legislature we turned our sights onto the cameras. Though business' use cameras to monitor or capture after the fact images of a crime, no one really watches over you. No one. If you ever need help don't rely on it to save you. Our concerned was at large; areas of crowds and stores should someone have one to be there to monitor activity. We filed a suit and won. If ever it goes into effect, it would be up to personal owners of business to use or disregard the record facts.

Now after years of living and reliving this past my time is at hand. I've been told I have stage 4 kidney cancer. Surgery is necessary. Too advanced for chemo or radiation to help at this point. But the type of evasive surgery that was used on me speed up my demise. It allowed it to spread so fast and the infection with it that I have succumb to it. I told Don I saw Jesus in my room at the hospital I saw his home in heaven. He was coming for me soon.

I never made it home. The MDA outlawed this procedure 2 months later.

Ellen passed away at 11:05 A.M., March 25, 2018.

Dereck Todd Lee Victims

Randi Merrier 28 yrs. old
  Murdered April 18, 1998

Gerra Wilson Green 41 yrs. old
  Murdered Sept 24, 2001

Geralyn Desoto 21 yrs. old
  Murdered Jan. 14, 2002

Charlotte Murray Pace 21 yrs. old
  Murdered May 31, 2002

Dione Alexander
  Survived: July 9, 2002

Pamela Kennermore 44 yrs. old
  Murdered July 12, 2002

Dene Colomb 23 yrs. old
  Murdered Nov 21, 2002

Carrie Lynn Yode
  Murdered March 3, 2003

Was also linked to another death

Connie Warner Zachary, Louisiana
  Murdered Aug 23, 1992

Announcement of the Commencement of DNA

Sampling from Arrestees
November 22, 2002, New Iberia, Louisiana

Sid Hebert, Sheriff of Iberia Parish, Louisiana
Ray Wickenheiser, Laboratory Director, Acadiana
Crime Lab, New Iberia, Louisiana
Tammy Pruet Northrup, Louisiana State
Police DNA Database Director
Captain Brian Wynne, Laboratory Director, Louisiana
State Police Crime Lab, Baton Rouge, Louisiana
Lt. Colonel John LeBlanc, Deputy
Superintendent, Louisiana State Police
Ellen Crawford Johnson, Survivor of Crime

<u>News Conference Announcement and Media Release</u>
Sheriff Sid Hebert
Iberia Parish Sheriff's Department
<u>Re: Announcement of the commencement of DNA sampling</u>
<u>from arrestees</u>

Sheriff Sid Hebert announced today that samples have been taken from individuals arrested for designated offenses, to be entered in the Louisiana State's new DNA Database. "As the President of the Acadiana Crime Lab Commission I felt compelled to lead the Sheriffs into the new millennium of crime detection when offered the chance. This marks the first time in Louisiana that individuals who are arrested will have their DNA sample included in a DNA database for wide comparison to crime scene DNA samples," said Sheriff Hebert. "Our concern is not only public safety in more quickly solving crimes now unsolved, but to focus our investigations and resources away from innocent individuals. Arrestee sampling will quickly widen the scope of our investigations to include far more individuals involved in the commission of crime."

Sheriff Hebert continued, "As the perpetrator is at large, many more crimes are often committed until law enforcement is able to develop the correct suspect and bring a sample of DNA to the lab. In the meantime, public safety is at risk. The ability to sample arrestees will serve as a huge benefit to law enforcement and public safety. The case of the serial killer loose in Baton Rouge serves as an excellent example. There is little doubt that this individual has been involved in crime previously, as he had broken into the victim's homes, taken some of their valuables, and left his DNA behind in the assaults. While a convicted offender DNA database is valuable, this person is currently on the loose, and therefore would not be caught in the net cast by a convicted offender's DNA. Sampling arrestees is the tool not only to solve this crime, but many others where law enforcement has been unable to develop suspects using more conventional means."

"We are very excited about the crime solving potential of arrestee DNA sampling," concluded Sheriff Hebert, "As DNA is capable of freeing the innocent as well as solving murders with no witness, it is often the voice for the disenfranchised and those with no voice at all. This logical step will help prevent anyone from being wrongfully convicted, prevent the unnecessary need of interviewing people not involved in the commission of the crime, and to increase public safety by solving crimes with no suspects."

A statement by Ellen Crawford Johnson, a victim of an abduction and brutal rape occurring in Lafayette and St. Martin parishes, will be made telling the story of her ordeal, and the role of DNA testing.

News Conference Announcement and Media Release
Ray Wickenheiser, Director
Acadiana Crime Lab
Re: Announcement of the commencement of DNA sampling from arrestees

Ray Wickenheiser, the Director of Acadiana Crime Lab in New Iberia, Louisiana stated, "The number of crimes solved is directly related to the number of samples from known individuals we can compare to crime scene DNA. The more DNA profiles in the database, the more crimes we solve. Forensic scientists have made great technological strides in our ability to obtain DNA profiles from crime scenes. However, if there is no known sample to compare to the crime scene sample, our hands are tied until the right sample comes in."

When asked about the dangers of DNA sampling with respect to arrestees having their rights violated, Ray Wickenheiser responded, "DNA samples are taken with an oral swab in a manner of seconds, with no harm to the individual. It is a felony for us to mishandle the samples by using DNA and information outside of its narrow crime-solving mandate.

Further, the areas of DNA we look at with forensics are non-coding DNA regions. This means the DNA is not used by the body to determine any part of our body's make-up. We cannot see the color of eyes, skin, or hair or any other medical information like genetic diseases. Other than giving us a "human serial number" which is outstanding for telling people apart, no other information is gained. I stress that our first purpose is to exclude a suspect individual. If just one DNA band of the 26 we observe is different, we can eliminate that suspect with 100% confidence. If all 26 of the bands match on the other hand, that is powerful evidence of a DNA source."

News Conference Talking Points
Re: Announcement of the commencement of DNA sampling from arrestees

In our war against crime, do you stick to hand to hand combat in the trenches, or do you use a missile in a surgical strike against a target?

This analogy applies today to our use of technology against the perpetrators of crime. Do we use only a labor-intensive door-to-door footwork approach, or do we apply the latest tools of technology like DNA testing?

Criminals strike against our citizens as surely as terrorists did on September eleventh. The difference is that the tragedies occur 1 at a time as opposed to 3000.

Recent statistics indicate that an average of over 366,000 sexual offenses occur in United States every year (source: U.S. Dept. of Justice, Bureau of Justice Statistics). That is every year averaged from since 1992 to 2000. Most rapes and sexual assaults against females were not reported to police. How many serial offenders are buried in that number, striking again and again until they are finally brought to justice?

Recidivism means repeating offenses, the nature of which generally increases in severity.

Recidivism (repeat offender) rates statistics are as follows (source: "Undetected Recidivism among Rapists and Child Molesters", Groth, Longo, McFadin, 1982):

Average age at first sexual offense:	18.8 years
Number of detected sexual offenses:	2.8
Undetected sexual offenses:	5.2
More than one offense:	67.1%

More than 2/3 of offenders commit multiple offenses, and most of them commit many offenses before they are caught. The state of Florida has a recidivism rate of 63% for all offenses. They have estimated the average number of sexual assaults per serial offender as being between 8 and 12 (source: David Coffman). It often takes 4 to 6 more sexual assaults for an offender to be first caught and convicted, and then have his DNA taken for a convicted offender DNA database. Once he is out, he then may commit another 4 to 6 more until he is apprehended the second time using DNA. This is where the arrestee DNA samples will help us move that clock forward, to catch that offender quickly, thus preventing many crimes, and saving many needless victims.

Offenses against children:

- 1 in 5 violent offenders serving time in state prison reported having victimized a child.
- 7 in 10 of these offenders reported that they were imprisoned for rape or sexual assault.
- More than 50% of the violent crimes against children involved victims 12 or younger.
- Source: U.S. Dept of Justice, Bureau of Justice Statistics, March 1996
- (http://www.ojp.usdoj.gov/ojs)

While this is clearly a public safety issue, it is much more. It is about using our resources more wisely. It is also about not wasting time bothering innocent people who are suspected of crime. Our goal is "to get it right the first time", because how many needless victims are too many? This is the right thing to do.

Overall, rape is the costliest
crime: With victim costs at
$127 billion, it exacts a
higher price than murder.
The Extent and Costs of Crime
Victimization: A New Look
National Institute of Justice

Rape in the U.S.

- Total of **500,000** sexual assaults on women*

  – Completed Rapes   170,000
  – Attempted Rape   140,000
  – Other Sexual Assault 190,000

- Attacker Unknown to Victim **1 in 3**

*Refers to persons age 12 or older
  Source: National Crime Victimization Survey
               Crimes Against Women: Estimates from the Redesigned
               Survey
               Prepared by the U.S. Dept. of Justice, Bureau of Justice
               Statistics, August 1995
               http://www.ojp.usdoj.gov/bjs/cvict.htm

Rape in the US – Individual Cost

- **Productivity** $2,200
- Medical Care $500
- Mental Health Care $ 2,200
- Police / Fire Services $ 37
- Social / Victim Services $27
- Property Loss / Damage $100
- Quality of Life $81,400

   TOTAL $87,000

**Source: "Victim Costs and Consequences: A New Look"
Miller, Cohen, and Weirsema National Institute of Justice,
January 1996**

Offenses Against Children

- **1 in 5** violent offenders serving time in state prison reported having victimized a child.
- **7 in 10** of these offenders reported that they were imprisoned for rape or sexual assault.
- **More than 50%** of the violent crimes against children involved victims 12 or younger.

Source: Child Victimizers: Violent Offenders and Their Victims Prepared by the U.S. Dept. of Justice, Bureau of Justice Statistics, March 1996
http://www.ojp.usdoj.gov/bjs

Estimated Cost by Offender

Average Societal Cost per Rape $87,000

Average Number of Rapes per Offender: 8-12

    Assume:

    Offender commits 8 Rapes:

    CODIS hit stops offender midway through, thus preventing 4 rapes

Then:

    4 prevented rapes @ *$87,000 per rape = $348,000

Source: "Victim Costs and Consequences: A New Look"
           Miller, Cohen, and Weirsema
           National Institute of Justice, January 1996
           http://www.ncjrs.org/txtfiles/victcost.txt

A Conservative Estimate

◆ CODIS has matched on approximately 100 sexual assault cases

◆ Assume: DNA hits prevent only 25% of those offenders from committing just one more assault:

  $87,000 * 25 rapes = $2,175,000

◆ Remember, the average offender commits 8-12 rapes!

Recidivism Rates

- Mean Age at First Offense   18.8
- Detected Sexual Assaults   2.8
- Undetected Sexual Assaults   5.2
- More than 1 Offense   67.1%

Source: "Undetected Recidivism among Rapists and
Child Molesters" Groth, Longo, McFadin, 1982

Recidivism Rates for Offenders Community Supervision

Murdered	13,200 people
Raped	13,000 people
Robbed	39,500 people
Burglarized	39,600 people
Assaulted	19,200 people
Stole	7,900 vehicles

Source: Bureau of Justice Statistics

They're On the Street...
Care, Custody, and Control of Convicted Sex Offenders

Source: "Sex Offenses and Offenders"
          Bureau of Justice Statistics, February 1997
          http://www.ojp.usdoj.gov/bjs

Why Burglary Convictions?

- There is a 67% recidivism rate among convicted sex offenders and the average number of sexual assaults per offender is 8.
- 56% of the offenders linked to sexual assaults and homicides by DNA Database matches have had prior burglaries.
- Collecting samples from offenders convicted of burglary could help insure their DNA profiles are in the Database <u>before</u> commission of their first violent act.

Criminal History of Offenders Linked to Sexual Assaults and Homicides

- 11%   Firearm possession
- 30%   Drug charge
- 34%   Grand Theft
- 34%   Robbery
- 56%   Burglary

Recidivism Rates for Offenders
Community Supervision

Murdered	13,200 people
Raped	13,000 people
Robbed	39,500 people
Burglarized	39,600 people
Assaulted	19,200 people
Stole	7,900 vehicles

Source: Bureau of Justice Statistics

Prisoners Convicted for Burglary: Past Criminal History

- 14% Homicide
- 9% Sexual Assault
- 13% Aggravated Battery
- 9% Lewd Acts
- 45% Total

Crimes for which DNA samples must be provided in Louisiana:

14:42-14:43.5

> Aggravated Rape
> Forcible Rape
> Simple Rape
> Sexual Battery
> Aggravated Sexual Battery
> Oral Sexual Battery
> Intentional Exposure to AIDS

14:80-14:81.2

> Felony Carnal Knowledge of a Juvenile
> Misdemeanor Carnal Knowledge of a Juvenile
> Indecent Behavior with Juvenile
> Pornography Involving Juveniles
> Molestation of A Juvenile

14:30-14:32.7

> First Degree Murder
> Second Degree Murder
> Manslaughter
> Negligent Homicide
> Vehicular Homicide
> Feticide
> First Degree Feticide
> Second Degree Feticide

14:34-14:38.2

Aggravated Battery
Second Degree Battery
Battery of a Police Officer
Battery of a School Teacher
Battery of a School or Recreation Athletic Contest Official
Battery of a Correctional Facility Employee
Disarming of a Peace Officer
Aggravated Second Degree Battery
Simple Battery
Simple Battery of a Child Welfare Worker
Simple Battery of the Infirm
Aggravated Assault
Assault by Drive-By Shooting
Aggravated Assault Upon a Peace Officer With a Firearm
Unlawful use of a laser on a police officer
Simple Assault
Aggravated Assault with a Firearm
Mingling Harmful Substances
Assault on a School Teacher

14:40.1-40.2

Terrorizing
Stalking

14:44-14:45

Aggravated Kidnapping
Second Degree Kidnapping
Simple Kidnapping

Statement by Ellen Crawford Johnson   November 22, 2002

Ladies and Gentlemen:

On behalf of myself and all victims of crime, I want to thank you for being here today.

I was 52 years old when my life was altered by crime. Altered in ways I could never have imagined, and still find hard to believe.

My life was perfectly normal before March 11, 2001. I worked 45 hours every week as a secretary; I shopped for groceries, clothing, and all the essentials for comfortable living; I visited antique stores to satisfy my passion for old treasure. In short, I was a healthy, energetic, vibrant human being.

It was around 9:15 a.m. on a sunny cool Sunday morning that my life was forever changed. With absolutely no warning, I was stabbed multiple times, robbed, and kidnapped from a Wal-mart parking lot is Lafayette, Louisiana. I fought the perpetrator for a full minute before he got me into my truck. He drove to St. Martin Parish, and in a remote area he raped me.

This person had been released from prison only two weeks before. I saved my life by jumping from the truck going over 50 miles per hour. I broke my left arm in two places, my left ankle was shattered because he ran over me after I hit the pavement, my right toe was broken, and my left shoulder and hip were dislocated. I was bedridden for 77 days, in a wheel chair for three months, and on a single crutch for 90 days.

The assailant was caught two days later still driving my husband's truck. I am sure he thought I was dead. The two ranchers who came to my rescue had actually thought I was a mannequin until I raised my head after hitting the pavement.

I was able to give a detailed description of the assailant. But, even with that, it was my word against his concerning the rape. This is why DNA testing is so wonderful. The DNA <u>proved</u> that the person I described was <u>indeed</u> the rapist.

After a person has been defiled as I was and many others have been before and since then, you feel like a shell of your former self. You so desperately want the monster caught - but then what? Without DNA testing to <u>prove</u> their guilt, you wonder if the authorities believe what you are saying. I thank God for all the wonderful technology we have available to us – and, on top of the list for me is DNA testing.

Since the kidnapping/rape I have been made to believe criminals have more rights than their victims.

Not only do victims suffer, their entire family suffers. My husband has suffered horribly since this happened; yet, he has not been short tempered with me, not once.

Alterations in my life? I have not driven <u>at all</u> since 3/11/01; I walk with a limp because my left leg is now shorter than my right, and my ankle is permanently damaged; my left shoulder is frozen because massive arthritis set up in the top break of my left arm; I have not been outside, even in my yard, by myself; last, but not least, I am absolutely terrified of all strangers.

It seems a lot of criminals feel their "rights" are violated by DNA sampling. Yet, you do not hear them object to fingerprinting. To me DNA is just another fingerprint.

In closing, I must pay homage to my Lord and Saviour, Jesus Christ. I asked him to deliver me that day, and he did. I am one of the most blessed of people. I must also say thank-you to the human being who developed DNA testing. I can sleep well at night, because the person who hurt me can <u>not</u> hurt another innocent human being. For that I am so thankful.

Sincerely,
Ellen Crawford Johnson

WEST'S LOUISIANA STATUTES UNANNOTATED
LOUISIANA REVISED STATUTES
TITLE 15. CRIMINAL PROCEDURE
CHAPTER 6-A. DNA DETECTION OF
SEXUAL AND VIOLENT OFFENDERS

'601. Short title

This Chapter shall be known as the "DNA Detection of Sexual and Violent Offenders Act".

'602. Legislative findings and objectives

The Louisiana Legislature finds and declares that DNA data banks are important tools in criminal investigations, in the exclusion of individuals who are the subject of criminal investigations or prosecutions, and in deterring and detecting recidivist acts. More than forty states have enacted laws requiring persons arrested for or convicted of certain crimes, especially sex offenses, to provide genetic samples for DNA profiling. Moreover, it is the policy of this state to assist federal, state, and local criminal justice and law enforcement agencies in the identification and detection of individuals in criminal investigations and in the identification of missing persons, to assist in the recovery or identification of human remains from disasters, and to assist with other humanitarian identification purposes. It is therefore in the best interest of the state to establish a DNA data base and a DNA data bank containing DNA samples submitted by individuals arrested, convicted, or presently incarcerated for felony sex offenses and other specified offenses.

'603. Definitions

For purposes of this Chapter, the following terms shall have the following meanings:

(1) "CODIS" means Combined DNA Index System, the Federal Bureau of Investigation's national DNA identification index system that allows the storage and exchange of DNA records submitted by state and local forensic DNA laboratories.

(2) "Criminal justice agency" means any criminal justice agency as defined in R.S. 15:576(3).

(3) "Deputy secretary" means the deputy secretary of the Department of Public Safety and Corrections, public safety services, or the commander of the Louisiana State Police.

(4) "DNA" means deoxyribonucleic acid, which is located in cells and provides an individual's personal genetic blueprint and which encodes genetic information that is the basis of human heredity and forensic identification

(5) "DNA record" means DNA identification information stored in the state DNA data base or the Combined DNA Index System for the purpose of generating investigative leads or supporting statistical interpretation of DNA test results. The DNA record is the result obtained from the DNA typing tests. The DNA record is comprised of the characteristics of a DNA sample which is of value in establishing the identity of individuals.

(6) "DNA sample" means a blood, tissue, or bodily fluid sample provided by any person with respect to offenses covered by this Chapter or submitted to the state police criminalistics laboratory pursuant to this Chapter for analysis or storage, or both.

(7) "FBI" means the Federal Bureau of Investigation.

(8) "Felony sex offense" means a felony offense or an attempt to

commit a felony offense in violation of R.S. 14:42 through 43.5 or R.S. 14:80 through 81.2.

(9) "Fund" means the DNA Detection Fund established in this Chapter.

(10) "Other specified offense" means a commission of the following:

    (a) A violation of R.S. 14:30 through 32.7.

    (b) A violation of R.S. 14:34 through 38.2.

    (c) A violation of R.S. 14:40.1 through 40.2.

    (d) A violation of R.S. 14:44 through 45.

(11) "State police" means the office of state police or the state police criminalistics laboratory.

'604. Powers and duties of state police

In addition to any other powers and duties conferred in this Chapter, the state police shall:

(1) Be responsible for the policy management and administration of the state DNA identification record system to support law enforcement agencies and other criminal justice agencies.

(2) Promulgate rules and regulations to carry out the provisions of this Chapter.

(3) Provide for liaison with the FBI and other criminal justice agencies in regard to the state's participation in CODIS or in any DNA data base designated by the state police.

'605. State DNA data base

There is hereby established the state DNA data base. It shall be administered by the state police and provide DNA records to the FBI for storage and maintenance by CODIS. The state DNA data base shall have the capability provided by computer software and procedures administered by the state police to store and maintain DNA records related to:

(1) Forensic casework.
(2) Offenders required to provide a DNA sample under this Chapter.
(3) Anonymous DNA records used for research or quality control.

'606. State DNA data bank

There is hereby established the state DNA data bank. It shall serve as the repository of DNA samples collected under this Chapter.

'607. State police recommendation of additional offenses

The state police may recommend to the legislature that it enact legislation for the inclusion of additional offenses for which DNA samples shall be taken and otherwise subjected to the provisions of this Chapter. In determining whether to recommend additional offenses, the state police shall consider those offenses for which DNA testing will have a substantial impact on the detection and identification of sex offenders and violent offenders.

'608. Procedural compatibility with FBI

The DNA identification system as established by the state police shall be compatible with the procedures specified by the FBI, including use of comparable test procedures, laboratory equipment, supplies, and computer software.

'609. Drawing or taking of DNA samples

A. A person who is arrested for a felony sex offense or other specified offense on or after September 1, 1999, shall have a DNA sample drawn or taken at the same time he is fingerprinted pursuant to the booking procedure.

B. Any person who is convicted or enters into a plea agreement resulting in a conviction on or after September 1, 1999, for a felony sex offense or other specified offense committed prior to that date shall have a DNA sample drawn as follows:

(1) A person who is sentenced to a term of confinement for an offense covered by this Chapter shall have a DNA sample drawn upon intake to a prison, jail, or any other detention facility or institution. If the person is already confined at the time of sentencing, the person shall have a DNA sample drawn immediately after the sentencing.

(2) A person who is convicted or enters into a plea agreement resulting in a conviction for an offense covered by this Chapter shall have a DNA sample drawn as a condition of any sentence that will not involve an intake into a prison, jail, or any other detention facility or institution.

(3) Under no circumstances shall a person who is convicted or enters into a plea agreement resulting in a conviction for an offense covered by this Chapter be released in any manner after such disposition unless and until a DNA sample has been withdrawn.

C. A person who has been convicted or enters into a plea agreement resulting in a conviction for a felony sex offense or other specified offense before September 1, 1999, and who is still serving a term of confinement in connection therewith on that date shall not be released in any manner prior to the expiration of his maximum term of confinement unless and until a DNA sample has been withdrawn.

D. All DNA samples taken pursuant to this Chapter shall be taken in accordance with regulations promulgated by the state police.

E. As used in this Section, the term "released" means any release, parole, furlough, work release, prerelease, or release in any other manner from a prison, jail, juvenile detention facility, or any other place of confinement.

'610. Procedures for withdrawal, collection, and transmission of DNA samples

A. Each DNA sample required to be drawn under this Chapter from persons who are arrested, incarcerated, or confined shall be drawn at the place of booking, incarceration, or confinement. DNA samples from persons who are not ordered or sentenced to a term of confinement shall be drawn or taken at a prison, jail unit, juvenile facility, or other facility to be specified by the court. Only those individuals qualified to draw or take DNA samples in a medically approved manner shall draw or take a DNA sample to be submitted for DNA analysis. The DNA sample and a set of fingerprints taken upon booking shall be delivered to the state police in accordance with state police rules and regulations.

B. A person authorized to draw or take DNA samples under this Chapter shall not be criminally liable for withdrawing a DNA sample and transmitting test results pursuant to this Chapter if he performed these activities in good faith and shall not be civilly liable for such activities when he acted in a reasonable manner according to generally accepted medical and other professional practices.

'611. Procedures for conduct, disposition, and use of DNA analysis

A. The state police shall prescribe procedures to be used in the collection, submission, identification, analysis, storage, and disposition of DNA samples and typing results of DNA samples submitted pursuant to this Chapter. The DNA sample typing results shall be stored in the state DNA data base and records of testing shall be retained on file with the state police.

B. The state police may contract with third parties to effectuate the purposes of this Chapter.

C. Except as otherwise provided in R.S. 15:612(C), the tests to be performed on each DNA sample shall be used only for law enforcement identification purposes or to assist in the recovery or identification of human remains from disasters or for other humanitarian identification purposes, including identification of missing persons.

D. Any other party contracting to carry out the functions of this Chapter shall be subject to the same restrictions and requirements of this Chapter, insofar as applicable, as apply to the state police, and subject to any additional restrictions imposed by the state police.

'612. DNA data base exchange

A. The state police shall receive, store, and perform analysis on DNA samples or contract for DNA typing analysis with a qualified DNA laboratory that meets the guidelines as established by the state police, and shall classify and file the DNA record of identification characteristic profiles of DNA samples submitted under this Chapter and make such information available as provided in this Section. The state police may enter a contract for the storage of DNA typing analysis and for DNA typing analysis with a qualified DNA laboratory that meets guidelines as established by the state police. The results of the DNA profile of individuals in the state DNA data base shall be made available:

(1) To criminal justice agencies or approved crime laboratories which serve these agencies.

(2) Upon written or electronic request and in furtherance of an official investigation of a criminal offense or offender or suspected offender.

B. The state police shall adopt guidelines governing the methods of obtaining information from the state DNA data base and procedures for verification of the identity and authority of the requestor.

C. The state police may create a separate population data base comprised of DNA samples obtained under this Chapter after all personal identification is removed. The state police may share or disseminate the population data base with other criminal justice agencies or crime laboratories that serve to assist the state police with statistical data bases. The population data base may be made available to and searched by other agencies participating in the CODIS system.

'613. Cancellation of authority to access or exchange DNA records

The state police, for good cause shown, may revoke or suspend the right of a forensic DNA laboratory within this state to access or exchange DNA identification records with criminal justice agencies.

'614. Removal of records

A. A person whose DNA record or profile has been included in the data base or data bank pursuant to this Chapter may request that his record or profile be removed on the following grounds:

(1) The arrest on which the authority for including his DNA record or profile was based does not result in a conviction or plea agreement resulting in a conviction.

(2) The conviction on which the authority for including his DNA record or profile was based has been reversed and the case dismissed.

B. The state police shall remove all records and identifiable information in the data base or data bank pertaining to the person and destroy all samples from the person upon receipt of a written request for the removal of the record and a certified court order of expungement properly obtained pursuant to the provisions of R.S. 44:9.

'615. Mandatory cost

Unless the defendant shows that undue hardship would result, a mandatory cost of two hundred fifty dollars, which shall be in addition to any other costs imposed pursuant to law, shall automatically be imposed on any person convicted of a felony sex offense or other specified offense, and all proceeds derived from this Section shall be transmitted to the fund.

'616. Confidentiality of records

Unless otherwise provided, all DNA profiles and samples submitted to the state police pursuant to this Chapter shall be confidential.

'617. Disclosure prohibited

A. Any person, by virtue of employment or official position, or any person contracting to carry out any functions under this Chapter, including any officer, employee, or agent of such contractor, who has possession of or access to individually identifiable DNA information contained in the state DNA data base or in the state DNA data bank shall not disclose it in any manner to any person or agency not authorized to receive it knowing that such person or agency is not authorized to receive it.

B. No person shall obtain individually identifiable DNA information from the state DNA data base or the state DNA data bank without authorization to do so.

'618. Criminal penalties

A. Any person who violates R.S. 15:617(A) shall be fined not more than five hundred dollars or imprisoned with or without hard labor for not more than six months, or both.

B. Any person who knowingly violates R.S. 15:617(B) shall be fined not more than five hundred dollars or imprisoned with or without hard labor for not more than six months, or both.

C. Any person who tampers or attempts to tamper with any sample of blood, tissue, or other bodily fluids or the collection container without lawful authority shall be fined not more than five hundred dollars or imprisoned with or without hard labor for not more than six months, or both.

'619. DNA Detection Fund

All monies collected as costs pursuant to R.S. 15:615 shall be deposited into the state treasury. After compliance with the requirements of Article VII, Section 9(B) of the Constitution of Louisiana relative to the Bond Security and Redemption Fund, and prior to monies being placed in the state general fund, an amount equal to that deposited as required in this Section shall be credited to a special fund hereby created in the state treasury to be known as the DNA Detection Fund. The monies in this fund shall be appropriated by the legislature to the state police to assist in carrying out the provisions of this Chapter. All unexpended and unencumbered monies in this fund at the end of the fiscal year shall remain in such fund. The monies in this fund shall be invested by the state treasurer in the same manner as monies in the state general fund and interest earned on the investment of monies shall be credited to this fund, again, following compliance with the requirements of > Article VII, Section 9(B) relative to the Bond Security and Redemption Fund.

'620. Authority of law enforcement officers

Nothing in this Chapter shall limit or abrogate any existing authority of law enforcement officers to take, maintain, store, and utilize DNA samples for law enforcement purposes.